INTO
JUPITER'S
WORLD

INTO JUPITER'S WORLD

BY ROBERT E. DUNBAR

8728
F
DUN

PHOTOGRAPHS BY JACK HAMILTON

Blairsville Junior High School
Blairsville, Pennsylvania

A GROLIER COMPANY

FRANKLIN WATTS
NEW YORK | LONDON | TORONTO | SYDNEY | 1981
A TRIUMPH BOOK

Photograph on p. 34 courtesy of
the Astronomical Society of the Pacific © 1979.
Photograph on p. 63 courtesy of
the U.S. Department of Commerce/National Oceanic
and Atmospheric Administration.

Library of Congress Cataloging in Publication Data

Dunbar, Robert E
Into Jupiter's world.

(A Triumph book)
SUMMARY: Four cadets leave Space Station Mars
bound for the Jupiter system to investigate
the source of some unusual radio signals.
[1. Science fiction] I. Hamilton, Jack D.
II. Title.
PZ7.D8945In   [Fic]   80-25526
ISBN 0-531-04266-9

R. L. 3.3 Spache Revised Formula

FOR MY SON, JESSE

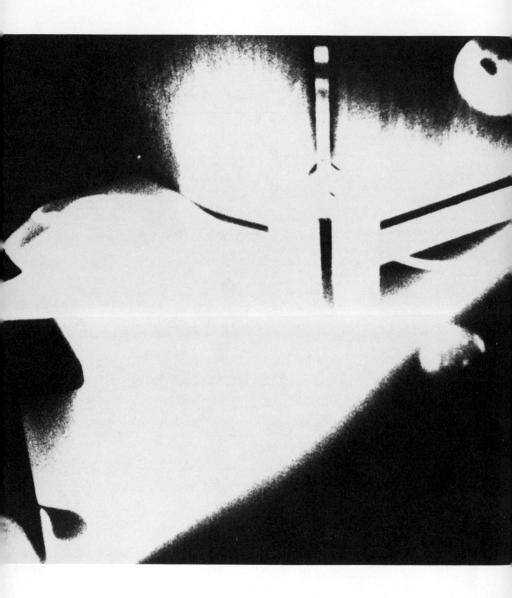

Blast off!

1
BLAST-OFF

Seventeen-year-old Will Pachek raced down the platform and hurried into the gleaming gray space shuttle. The lights on the craft were blinking. That meant it was ready for lift-off. Will dropped his gear into a floor locker. He then settled into a seat cube nearby. Just at that moment the shuttle door slid firmly shut, and a voice from the intercom barked "Hold onto your hats, cadets. We're up, up, and away!"

Immediately Will felt the sudden thrust of the shuttle's powerful engines as the ship began its climb upward through the Martian atmosphere, its destination Docking Station 3 and the spaceship *Alpha.* At first the roar of the engines was deafening. But soon the noise settled down to a low hum.

Will took his first look around. There were three other passengers in the chamber. Like himself, they were all seated on cubes. All wore the customary green and tan space patrol training suits. Two were girls, around the same age as Will. The other was a boy, a bit younger. Will introduced himself.

"Hi. I'm Will Pachek," he said smiling.

One of the girls quickly returned his smile. "I'm Kris Winter," she said. "This is Dora Johnson."

Dora glanced up at Will without smiling and offered a polite but cool "hello."

Turning to the junior member of the crew, Will asked him his name. "Radames Orestes," the boy said, also unsmiling. "Know what this mission is all about?" he asked Will.

"Only that we're heading for one of Jupiter's moons. That's all my squad leader would tell me. How about you?"

Will (left) talks with Dora and Radames.
It seems none of them know
much about the mission.

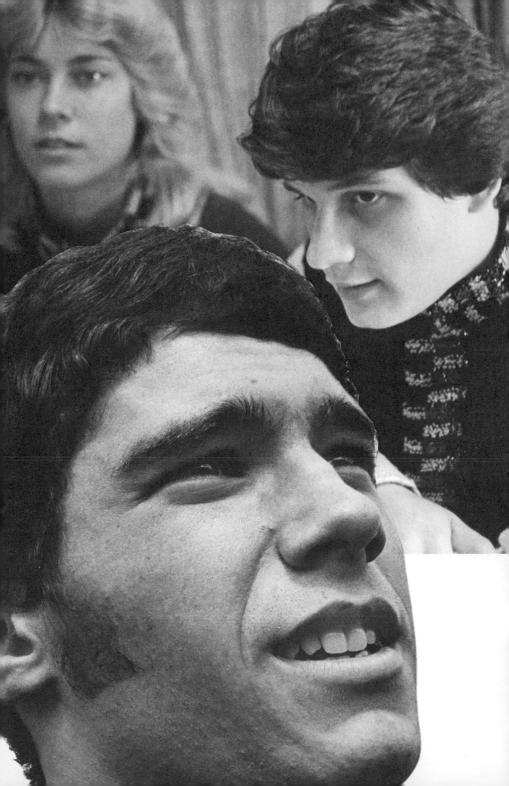

Dora Johnson cut in. "That's all we know, too. But it won't be a pleasure trip. Not with Captain Milo in command."

"So I've heard," Will said. "They call him the Twenty-first Century Terror! Where was your last mission?"

"Kris and I are just back from 'Moon Bust.' Three months of sifting through volcanic ash in the Mare Nostrum. It'll take us another three months to wash the dust out of our pores." She looked down at her hands and rubbed them in disgust.

"Where were you last?" Kris asked Will.

"Right here on good ole Space Station Mars. I was taking the 'nuts and bolts' test. We had to tear apart a space shuttle and then rebuild it." He chuckled. "We spent most of the month looking for missing parts or parts put in the wrong place—purposely. But we finally got it back together. Then we made a test run to Docking Station 1." He turned to Radames. "How about you?"

Radames squirmed in his seat for a moment. Then he said, "I just finished a space dynamics course. At Denver Academy. We did fly once to Earth's moon, but it was only a reconnaissance flight. No landing."

The other cadets glanced at each other for a moment. Then Kris said quickly, "Well, I can't say you missed much. The moon is nothing but rocks, holes, and dust, *buckets* of dust—"

A dull thud broke their conversation. The shuttle, which had been slowing down, came to a sudden stop and locked into its mooring.

Before any of the cadets could comment, a gruff voice announced on the intercom, "Cadets. Prepare to disembark. Prepare to disembark." The shuttle door slid open. Standing there was a tall, youthful-looking man in an officer's uniform.

The officer studied the cadets with cool, curious eyes as they recovered their gear from the lockers and filed out of the shuttle, directly into the hold of the huge spaceship. As soon as they had all gathered, he said, "Welcome aboard *Alpha.* I'm Lieutenant Farragut. As I read your names, please identify yourselves."

They did. The lieutenant then checked off their names from a list on a clipboard he held in his hands.

"Good. All accounted for. Leave your gear bags against the wall and follow me. Captain Milo wants to see you before you get squared away."

"Welcome aboard. I'm Lieutenant Farragut,"
the officer said, as he studied the cadets coolly.

Soon they were all heading down a long, narrow corridor to a waiting elevator. In just seconds they arrived two levels above the hold. As the elevator door slid open, they could see directly ahead of them a clear plastiglass wall. Behind it were two men. One, seated at an elaborate control panel, was in his mid-forties and handsome. But both his face and manner were stern. The insignia on his coat made his rank clear. He was the captain. Standing beside the captain, showing him a flight report, was a younger man, bald but with a large black moustache.

Farragut advanced to the intercom and announced the cadets' arrival. Without even turning to look, the captain motioned them to come in. A panel in the wall slid upward. The group filed silently inside.

The cadets remained at attention as the captain continued talking to the other officer. Finally he broke off, rose from his chair, and walked over to the cadets.

"At ease," he instructed, "and welcome aboard. At this moment you're standing in the Command Chamber. I'm Captain Milo. *Alpha* is going to be your home for six months, so we might as well begin to get acquainted, eh?"

Captain Milo

He studied each of the cadets' faces. Then he looked at Will and said, "You must be Pachek."

"Yes, sir."

"My report tells me you had some trouble with mechanics. Morrisey, here, is our Space Systems Controller. It'll be his job to make you an expert before this trip is over. Which one is Johnson?"

Dora identified herself.

"My report on you is the best of the lot, at least as far as exobiology goes. We have some rock samples from Ganymede aboard. We want you to analyze them. Let us know if there are any signs of life, past or present. Winter will assist you." He nodded at Kris. That left only Radames still to be recognized.

"Orestes," he said, turning to look squarely into the face of the young cadet, "since you've never been on a space mission before, you'll be working closely with Pachek and Morrisey for most of the trip."

"Yes, sir," Radames answered.

The captain seemed about to dismiss them when Will spoke up. "Sir, could you tell us something about the mission? All we know so far is that we're heading for the Jupiter system."

Milo remained silent for a moment. Then

he spoke. "Our mission is to investigate the source of some unusual radio signals. Space Command hasn't been able to identify them. We'll be landing on Callisto, one of Jupiter's moons. You'll get a fuller briefing later. That's all. Dismissed."

As the cadets filed out of the Command Chamber, they heard the captain tell Morrisey, "Prepare for blast-off."

2
TESTING

Mars soon became a small red ball in the distance as *Alpha* hurtled through space at a cruising speed of 260,000 kilometers per hour. It would take them three months to reach Callisto.

Kris and Dora set to work immediately. They would be running tests on rock samples from some of Jupiter's sixteen moons. Dora placed a rock specimen in the laser slicer. It cut the rock into thin strips. She gave some strips to Kris, who would examine them under a high-powered microscope. Dora would be conducting chemical tests with her samples.

"Well, at least we know what Captain Milo looks like now," Kris said.

"And we have an idea of what this mission is all about," Dora responded. At that moment she dropped a rock slice into a small tank half filled with a liquid solution. She also set a timer.

"Ganymede, oh, Ganymede, beautiful moon of Jupiter. Tell us your secrets," she chanted like a witch murmuring over a magic brew.

"And some of Captain Milo's too," Kris added with a laugh.

"What do you think of Will, Dora?" Kris asked suddenly.

"He's okay."

"I thought the captain was a bit rough on him—about the problem with mechanics, I mean," Kris said. "Even the experts could have trouble putting a space shuttle back together again."

"Maybe they had more trouble than Space Command expected."

"Maybe."

Dora leaned against the counter. "I wonder why they picked Radames for this mission. He's so young. And no experience to speak of. You and I have had several missions. Will too. And Rad seems so nervous, so unsure of himself."

"Like you and I were a few years ago." Kris paused a moment, then said, "I wonder what we'll find on Callisto. Whatever it is, it'll probably be rocky and hard, like Earth's moon." She sighed. "Oh, well. At least maybe it won't be dry. And we won't have to fight any dust storms!"

"Callisto may be drier than you think, Kris. Cold, but dry. Anyway, whatever we find, I hope it's friendly. Space Command has been on red alert for more than a month now because of communications blackouts between Saturn and Jupiter. They think it's some kind of electrical disturbance on Callisto. But they don't know what's causing it."

"Maybe the trouble is on Jupiter."

"Let's hope not. We can't land there to find out. It's just a big ball of gas! And the radiation would kill us before we even got close."

The two turned back to their experiments. Dora went over to a cabinet. She took three vials of different colored chemicals from it and put small portions of each into separate tanks. Then she watched and took notes. Kris studied her rock sample under the microscope and also took notes. The room became very quiet as the two concentrated on their work.

Two hours later, they took a break.

"Find anything interesting?" Kris asked.

"Nothing I didn't expect to find—at least so far. Mostly iron, with large amounts of hydrogen and helium. How about you?"

"I'd say this rock sample is billions of years

old. And I'm not sure, but I think I see traces of something. It might be the fossil of some organism."

"Really?" Dora asked. "Ganymede is supposed to be as dead as Earth's moon. Let me have a look."

Dora moved over to the microscope and studied the sample intently for a few moments. Then she said, "I think I see what you mean. Something there looks like it could be part of a worm or a beetle slug." She rose from her chair. "I'm going to check through some slides in the Databank Resource File."

"Okay," said Kris.

After a while Dora returned. She was carrying a small box of slides. She and Kris took out a few and compared them to the Ganymede sample. There were similarities. But there were also differences.

"Ganymede may be dead now," Kris said at last. "But it looks like it might have been alive at one time."

"Or still is—in spite of what most scientists believe," Dora said. She was silent for a moment as they both turned this possibility over in their minds. Suddenly Dora stood up. "How about going to the lounge for some coffee?"

"Terrific idea," Kris responded heartily.

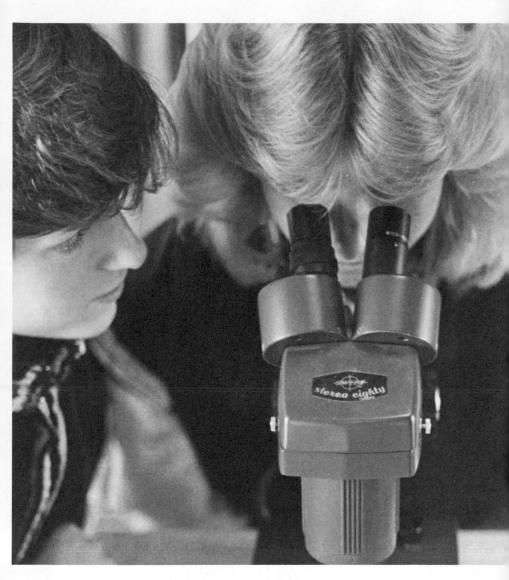

Dora examines the slide under the microscope. Kris looks on.

Back in the lounge, Kris poured two cups of coffee. She was handing one to Dora when Will came in.

"Well," he said, "I see I'm just in time. Got a cup for me?"

Kris filled another cup and handed it to Will. They all sat down.

"Where's Radames?" Dora asked.

"Oh, he'll be along. Controller Morrisey gave him some extra chores. He's taking inventory in the storeroom. Wanted to finish it today."

"Doesn't he need your help? Or have you gotten time off for good behavior?" asked Dora.

"Actually, I'm on my way to see Lieutenant Farragut. Captain Milo's orders. But Morrisey said I could stop for some coffee first."

They settled into a quiet mood, each thinking his or her own thoughts. But that ended abruptly as the intercom suddenly crackled and came to life. "General briefing. Five minutes. Control Chamber." It was Captain Milo's voice.

The three arrived together on schedule. They found Morrisey and Radames already there. Captain Milo looked troubled. He spoke even more briskly than usual.

"I've just been in contact with Space Station Mars," he said. "There's been another dysfunction in radar-compute in the area of Saturn.

The cadets enjoy a few relaxing moments in the lounge. They are soon summoned, however, to the Control Chamber.

The blackout lasted twelve hours. The spaceship patrolling Saturn had to return to base."

He paused to let the message sink in. He could see a question beginning to form on the cadets' faces.

"This will not affect our mission—at least for the time being. Space Command wants us to continue our run to Callisto. But we've got to keep a close watch on radar-compute. Flying blind in outer space can be quite hazardous."

He looked at Will. "Pachek will be the first to get lessons on how to work radar-compute. Farragut will instruct him."

He shifted position. "Any machine can have a minor breakdown and be fixed again without much trouble. The crew members aboard the Saturn spaceship are expert. I've been on missions with them. I believe their report. Some outside force was at work, blocking their radar-compute. No one knows how or why. That's all." They were dismissed.

Will joined Farragut immediately for his first session with radar-compute. The others went back to their own tasks. But one thing was now clear to all of them. They could no longer take that vital instrument for granted. The mission—maybe even their lives—depended on its proper functioning.

3
ALPHA'S HEART

Alpha sped through space like a silver bullet in a black void. In the far, far distance the brightness of Jupiter and its satellites beckoned.

All of the space cadets eventually learned how radar-compute worked. After the lessons were over, Will and Radames continued working with Controller Morrisey in the Space Dynamics Lab. Dora and Kris resumed their work in the Exobiology Lab.

Immediately below the Space Dynamics Lab were *Alpha*'s powerful atomic engines, the heart of the spaceship. On the level above was the Control Chamber, Captain Milo's station and *Alpha*'s brains.

Morrisey was giving Will and Radames a

complete knowledge of *Alpha* and its landing vehicle, *L-7*. *L-7* would be used in the descent to Callisto's surface.

In the lab were working models of *Alpha* and *L-7*. The landing vehicle showed flexible, spiderlike legs. These legs could adjust to any surface and maintain a level position, even on a hillside. The lander's numbers were painted boldly in yellow on its black body. Morrisey referred to the *L-7* affectionately as "Elsa."

As they studied the complexities of spaceship *Alpha,* Will grew increasingly amazed. It was the most advanced ship in the Space Patrol fleet. In fact, it was the first of a new line; hence, the name "Alpha." It could operate in space almost indefinitely. There was a "greenhouse" section where fresh food was grown in continuous cycles. Solar energy was captured and intensified to speed up the process. An atmospheric converter swallowed gusts of solar wind and produced a ready supply of water for the ship. One large room contained lockers with a year's supply of frozen meat. The cooking was computerized. This eliminated the need for cooks. Ripe vegetables were picked, cleaned, and cooked by machine. The menu for each of the 180 days of the mission was preprogrammed into the computer.

Living conditions aboard *Alpha* were nearly as comfortable as they were on Mars. Every physical need had been provided for. Each crew member had a small sleeping room with a sink, toilet, and shower. There were two lounges, one for the officers and the other for the space cadets. There the crew could relax, play games, read, or watch movies—when not on duty. The entire crew took their meals together in a large dining room. They exercised using the equipment and swimming pool in the spacious recreation room right next door to the dining room.

Alpha's speed was remarkable. It was the fastest ship in the Space Patrol's awesome fleet. It also excelled in communications. Radio and television signals could be relayed to Space Station Mars in just minutes. This would be true even when *Alpha* went into orbit around Callisto, some 500 million kilometers distant.

Controller Morrisey told Will and Radames these things and more with a certain amount of pride. But he was quick to point out that *Alpha* was not infallible. Things could go wrong. The atmospheric converter, which adjusted the engine's use of fuel, was sensitive to shock and other interferences. Radar-compute was also delicate. The engines themselves could malfunction, break down. There was an auxiliary engine, of course. But it was designed for temporary use only, while repairs on the other engines were being made.

One morning while lecturing on such matters in the Space Dynamics Lab, Morrisey abruptly stopped speaking. Will and Radames waited for him to continue.

"Did you fellows happen to look at the Log this morning?" he finally asked. This was part of daily routine. Both Will and Radames were expected to note all entries in the Space Log Morrisey kept.

"Sure," Will answered. "Just like always. Why?"

"Did you notice anything special about today's entry?"

Radames broke in. "It said we were now entering the Asteroid Belt."

"That's right," Morrisey said, "the Asteroid Belt. Now what does that mean to you? Will, you answer."

Will thought for a moment. "Well, for one thing it means we're getting closer to Callisto.

Rad tries to think of an
answer to Morrisey's question.

It also means we're in an active zone. We're passing through thousands of orbiting asteroids."

"Anything else? Rad?"

"Well . . ." Radames began, "with *Alpha*'s superb machinery it shouldn't be any problem, should it? I mean, radar-compute will guide us through without any problem."

"We hope so, Rad. At least that's the plan. But bear in mind we're now entering a fail-safe area of our mission. In other words, we're safe— if we don't fail." He smiled at his own joke. Behind the smile, though, was a look of real concern.

"What could go wrong?" Will asked. "There's been no problem with radar-compute in this area, only near Saturn."

"Nothing could go wrong," Morrisey said. "And then again, anything."

They soon resumed the day's discussion, which was about *L-7*. *L-7—Elsa*—was every bit as sophisticated as *Alpha* but on a much smaller scale. *Alpha* was the mother ship. *Elsa* could be directed by *Alpha* or operate independently.

Morrisey also reviewed the use of the rocket belts and space suits. The cadets would be wearing these on Callisto. Rocket-belt velocity ranged from 5 to 500 kilometers per hour.

Acceleration was controlled by a row of buttons on the "fore" side of the belt. The small but powerful rockets providing the power were mounted on the "aft" side. The rocket belts added only 60 kilograms to a person's body weight.

Each space suit contained several lightweight oxygen units with atmospheric converters. A heat device to maintain body warmth and waste discharge units to take care of this need were also attached. So were instruments to measure air temperature, radioactivity, electromagnetic force, and gravity. The suits had built-in compasses and odometers.

A transparent mask of very thin plastiglass fitted comfortably over the face. Lying against the throat was an electrovibrator. This device amplified and relayed sounds. With it the space cadets could communicate with each other.

As the day's work ended, Will and Radames headed for the lounge. Kris and Dora were already there. There was half an hour before dinner.

"Hi, space monkeys. Keeping the machine well oiled?" Kris greeted them.

"Funny," answered Will. "If we needed oil, we'd all be out of luck." Oil hadn't been available since the turn of the twenty-first century. Hydrogen-helium derivatives were the latest replacements. "How about you? Find any creepy crawlies today?"

"We're having them for dinner," Dora announced, and said it with such a straight face that the others stared at her in horror for a moment. Then they started laughing.

Just as Will and Radames were about to settle into chairs, a sudden rumble shook the room. There was an overpowering lurch, and the room seemed to capsize. They were all thrown to the floor. Furniture overturned. Plastiglass cups that Dora and Kris had filled with beverages spilled over and rolled against the wall. Then the room seemed to try to right itself, but it remained at a tilt. Gradually, however, the vibrations grew less violent.

Through the loudspeaker in the lounge the voice of Morrisey bellowed, "Pachek and Orestes! Report to Space Dynamics at once! Report to Space Dynamics at once!"

Will and Rad raced down the corridors, adjusting as best they could to the slanting floors and walls. They reached the lab in seconds. As they pulled open the door, they found themselves face to face with Captain Milo.

4
THE FIRST SCAR

"Come in, come in," the captain said impatiently. "Morrisey tells me we've been hit. By an asteroid. The left forward engine has something of a bruise. That's why we've lost our equilibrium. We've also been thrown off our flight path."

"Flight path?" Will asked, clearly shaken.

"Yes. It seems we're now heading for Io. Right planet, wrong moon! It could be worse. The impact could have thrown us into a complete reverse, back to Space Station Mars. Or out of the solar system entirely."

Morrisey jumped in. "Captain Milo wants you to help with engine repairs. We'll start immediately. Orestes, grab Kit A from the storeroom. Then get into your space suit. The solar wind can be unfriendly to humans. Pachek and I will meet you back here in ten minutes."

Radames went to the storeroom and found the kit on the shelves. It was very heavy. The weight of it made his right shoulder sag. By the time he returned to the lab, suited up, Will and Morrisey were already there. They were in their suits too and ready to go. Captain Milo had returned to the Control Chamber.

Morrisey pressed a button in the wall. A portion of the floor slid open, revealing a series of steps leading down to the engine rooms. Morrisey took the lead. Will and Radames followed.

The forward engine room was cramped. They had to walk hunched over to keep from hitting their heads on the ceiling.

As they entered the chamber, Will noted the oxygen reading. Zero! The asteroid had actually knocked a small chunk out of the side of the ship! The airless and icy solar wind was whipping through the room. To breathe it would mean instant death. Morrisey was right. Apparently *Alpha*—in spite of its advanced design—was not without flaws.

As Morrisey and Will moved ahead to examine the damage, Radames hesitated. The dark void of space could clearly be seen through the hole. It was unnerving. Radames found he was shaking. His heart was racing. He didn't know if he could go any farther.

He took a few deep breaths. That helped. Then he forced himself to take a few steps, and then a few more. In a moment, he had caught up with Will and Morrisey, who were busy examining the hole.

"Pachek, we'll have to patch this right away," Morrisey was saying, "before the solar wind does any serious damage to the reactor. Orestes," he said, turning to Radames, "get me a sheet of replacement plate from the kit. Grade 11. The 2-meter size. And the helium torch."

Radames searched the kit for the requested materials. He was sweating heavily. His clear plastiglass face mask was blurred by moisture. Will noticed and looked at him questioningly. But Rad refused to meet his eyes. As soon as he had given Will the equipment, he sank back against the wall, his face turned away from the gaping hole.

Will held the heavy plate in place over the hole while Morrisey worked the torch. With the touch of an expert, Morrisey trimmed the plate perfectly. Then he applied just the right pres-

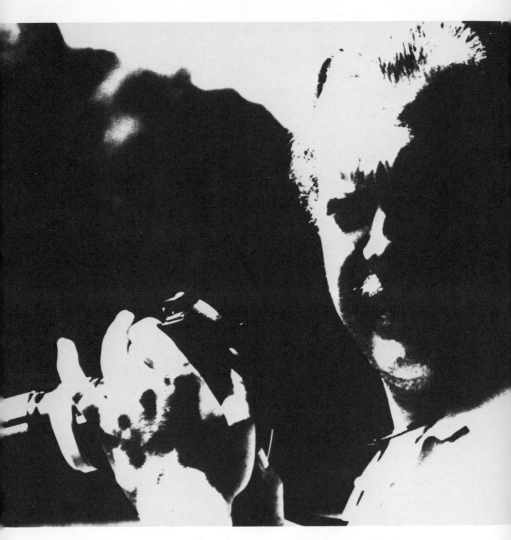

Morrisey trims the heavy plate.
The gaping hole left by the asteroid
is now completely sealed.

sure to form a heavy seam, actually melting the plate into the side of the chamber. After finishing, the two joined Radames to take a brief rest before examining the engine for possible damage.

"Good work, boys," Morrisey said. "That should take care of that problem." Radames looked down at the floor. Will said nothing.

The damage to the engine, they soon discovered, was minor. A broken turbine ring and connecting rod were causing a reduction in power. Both parts were smashed beyond repair. They would have to be replaced. Morrisey turned the power off and sent Will to get new parts from the storeroom.

Will soon returned with the parts. Morrisey deftly removed the broken ring and rod and replaced them. Then he pushed the switch that returned full power to the engine.

"Well, boys, let's see if we did the job right, eh?" The engine responded with a powerful roar. Then it modulated to a loud hum. As it did this, the group could feel the spaceship right itself. It was a great relief to be level again.

Two hours later they all gathered in the Control Chamber to hear Captain Milo's report.

"We're now operating at full speed again. But we must get back on our original flight path.

Fortunately, Io is relatively close to Callisto. By this time tomorrow we should be at our destination. Dismissed!"

The four cadets headed for the lounge. It was still early. There was some time to relax before lights out. But there was uneasiness in the air. Nobody said anything. Yet a question on all their minds was, just how close had they come to being killed? And also, once they reached their objective, what new dangers would they find?

5
THE SOURCE

Breaking out of the flight path to Io was a challenge for *Alpha*'s command computer. Jupiter had sixteen moons. There was always the chance that escaping from Io might only fling them into the path of another moon—or worse.

Radar-compute had not prevented the collision in the Asteroid Belt. Of course, thousands of asteroids orbited that zone. Still. . . .

Morrisey had a theory to explain the failure. A small asteroid must have been hidden behind a larger one. This was why the small one—the one that hit—hadn't shown up on radar-compute. At least it hadn't appeared in time to prevent the collision. If Captain Milo had a different theory, he kept it to himself.

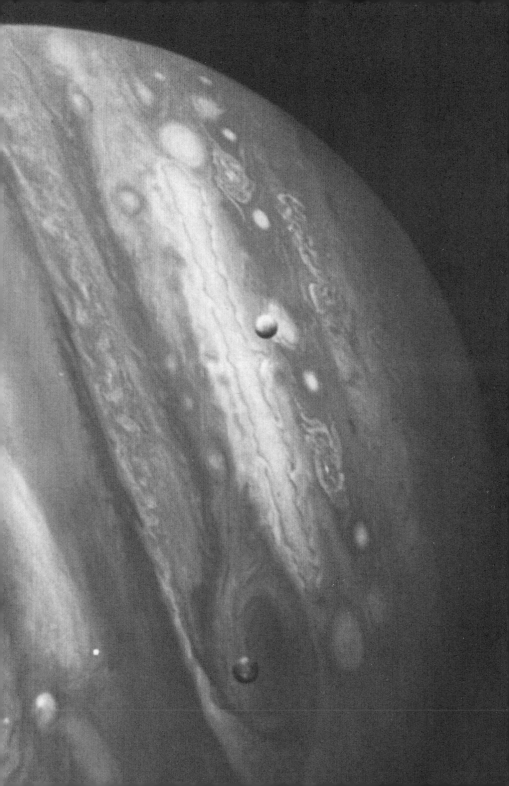

Jupiter's many moons proved to be no problem. *Alpha* went into orbit around Callisto the following day, as scheduled.

As soon as orbit was achieved, the cadets were called together for a briefing. It was almost three months to the day since they had blasted off from Space Station Mars. Will mentioned this to Dora on their way to the Control Chamber.

"What the captain wants, the captain gets," Dora answered with a shrug.

Upon entering the Control Chamber, they were greeted by a series of high-pitched sounds. Captain Milo had the radio wave receiver on full blast. Farragut and Morrisey were with him. So were Kris and Radames. Captain Milo motioned to Will and Dora to sit down.

The high-pitched sounds continued in an irregular pattern. Occasionally the bleep would drop to a lower register. But the intervals remained irregular. Will noted that Farragut and Radames were taking notes. After a few minutes, Captain Milo turned the receiver down.

Jupiter and its many
moons loom near.

"Well, Lieutenant, what do you make of it?"

Farragut looked up from his notes. "Well, the pattern is clearer, now that we're closer to the source, Captain. And the sounds are sharp and loud. But if they mean anything, I don't know what. I've compared them to all standard patterns—in fact to all known radio codes. They don't resemble anything we're familiar with."

Captain Milo turned to Radames. "Anything you can add to that Orestes?"

Radames moved nervously in his seat. "Well, sir," he began, "there are certain sound patterns that occur more frequently than others. Maybe they stand for the letter *e*. That's the most commonly used letter in our language. Why don't we separate all the sound patterns, then count how often they're used in a half-hour interval? Then we can compare them to the frequency of letters used in our language. That might give us a clue."

"That's just what I want you to do," the captain replied. He turned to the others. "We're now passing over the area of Callisto where the radio signals seem to be coming from. Some of us are going to explore that area. Pachek and Johnson, you'll go down with me in the landing vehicle. Farragut and Orestes will stay here on *Alpha* and continue working on the radio code. Winter will assist Morrisey in the Control Chamber."

"All the gear has been packed aboard *Elsa,* Captain," Morrisey said. "We're now one hundred kilometers above Callisto. The trip down will take about fifteen minutes."

Two hours later Will, Dora, and Captain Milo were locked into seat cubes on *L-7.* Their gear was behind them, in a tightly sealed compartment.

The confined space of *Elsa* was in sharp contrast to the giant, buildinglike mother ship, *Alpha. Elsa* was even smaller than the space shuttle that had brought them to *Alpha.*

Morrisey guided *Elsa* to a safe landing on Callisto just sixteen minutes after takeoff. *Elsa*'s spiderlike legs easily adjusted to the rough ground. The landing area was hard and strewn with rocks. Through *Elsa*'s windows, the crew had their first close look at Callisto's surface. They could see an unending stretch of dark, reddish-brown terrain, with occasional patches of frost. In the distance were mountains. Turbulent winds kept the surface in constant motion. This produced ripples in the low, wet areas.

In the distance, mountains could be seen.

The sky was a dim yellow. It was like the "first light" that precedes sunrise on Earth. Thin red and yellow clouds moved swiftly across the sky above. But there was no sign of vegetation anywhere. The terrain was as stark as a desert.

When their face masks were firmly in place, Captain Milo threw open the door of the lander. He checked his gasometer. The reading for oxygen was 10 percent. For carbon dioxide it was 20 percent. For hydrogen it was 60 percent. The rest was a mixture of helium, ammonia, methane, and other gases.

The readings were different from what Space Command had led them to expect. But this was Space Patrol's first manned landing on Callisto. The ground was not as wet as they had expected it to be either, at least not in this particular region. It was more like the frozen mud of early spring on Earth. But this was only the beginning. Eventually they would send back a detailed report on everything they saw.

At Captain Milo's signal, they put on their rocket belts. Then they filed out of the lander, the captain leading the way. Gale force winds greeted them. When they stepped on the frosty ground, they could feel a slight skidding sensation. But they had come prepared for Callisto's slippery icy stretches. In the soles of their boots was a layer of charged gas. This made traveling by foot quite safe. It was almost like walking on air, though their boots did leave an imprint on the surface. Callisto's gravity, not much stronger than Earth's, did not restrain their movement.

"Anyone for a swim?" Dora called out. "There must be a swimming hole carved somewhere in all this ice!"

Captain Milo was silent. He was getting his bearings. In one of his gloves he held a radiometer. It showed the strength and direction of the radio signals. Behind his face mask his eyes were intense with concentration. He turned to Will.

"The radio signals seem to be coming from a point about fifty kilometers northwest of here. We'll call it Point X. You and Johnson advance to that point. I'll join you after I check with Morrisey and run some tests. Radar-compute may have more information about the exact location. Evidently the source of the signals is somewhere within a hundred kilometers of our present position. It may be only an electrical disturbance on the surface that's causing the radio signals. But we won't know until we've had a look." With this the captain turned back to the ship.

In seconds the cadets had vaulted into the atmosphere. The roar of their rockets faded quickly behind them as they headed for Point X. Will led the way. Nearly half an hour went by before they reached the spot. Before descending, they circled the area in a wide arc, looking for clues to the source of the radio signals. They kept circling lower and lower. Soon they were only thirty meters above the ground.

Like the spot where *Elsa* had landed, this area was flat lowland, with occasional ravines. In the distance, however, they could see a mountain range with strange, greenish-yellow matter at its base. It reminded Will of giant coral reefs. The substance, whatever it was, was swaying. It was being tossed to and fro by the turbulent winds.

The surface below them was a continuation of rock-strewn desert. But the ground seemed more solid here. The only unusual feature was a large hole or crater in the side of a narrow ravine. It was a short distance from where they hovered in space. Will signaled to Dora, and they landed.

The landing was bumpy and the ground uneven. They helped each other remove their rocket belts for easier mobility. Dora helped Will remove his belt first. Then he removed

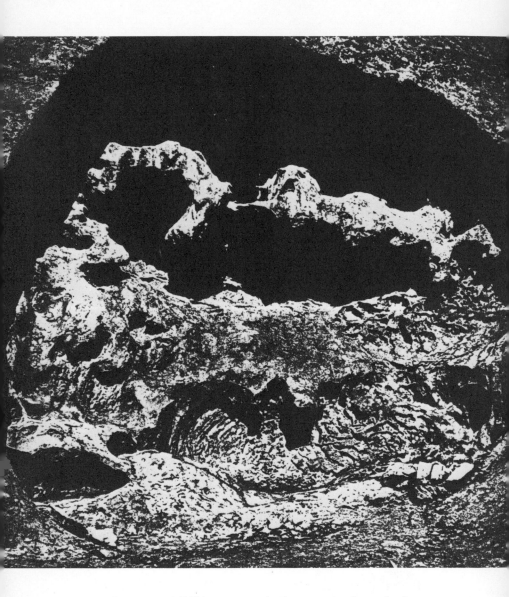

Dora and Will approach the mysterious hole.

hers. As he did so, Dora pointed to the large hole, which was about a hundred meters from them.

"Let's take a closer look at that hole," she said.

"Okay," Will responded. "But let's leave our rocket belts here. And first we'd better report to Captain Milo."

Using his communicator, Will alerted Captain Milo to what they had found. He gave the captain their exact position.

Captain Milo's voice came in clear and sharp. "Okay, you can approach the hole. But proceed *cautiously*. Report back to me as soon as you've had a look. I'll be here running some soil and atmosphere tests. That's all!" The communication came to an end.

As they stood there, the wind howled around them. It was much stronger here than it was where *Elsa* had landed. It was approaching the force of a hurricane.

Once released from the weight of the rocket belts, Will and Dora found it difficult to keep their balance in the high winds. The wind was blowing them in the direction of the hole. There seemed to be layers of swirling ground fog above the hole. As they started forward, the

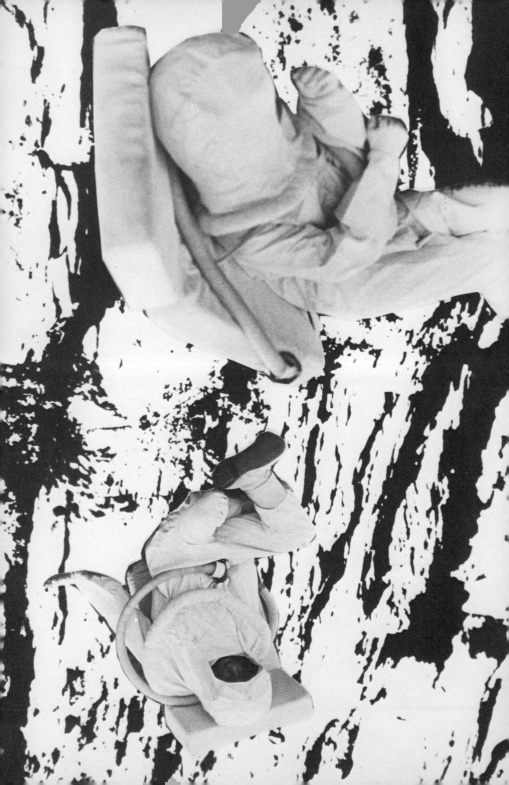

wind pushed them toward the hole with increasing force. Will glanced at his radiometer. The needle was at the uppermost limit of its measuring capacity. The radio signals still came from a northeast direction.

Will again led the way, with Dora a few steps behind him. When they were within twenty meters of the hole, Dora stumbled and fell. As Will stooped to help her to her feet, there was a sudden force of wind that lifted them both off the ground and toward the center of the hole. Clouds of yellow-tinged air were swirling around the hole and rushing down into it. Suddenly they were trapped in the vortex of the wind. They were being turned around in mid-air, faster and faster, and pulled down into the hole by an irresistible force!

Trapped in the vortex
of the wind!

6
THE BRIGHT PRISON

Down, down, down they plummeted, beneath Callisto's surface, tightly bound in the funnel of swirling air. As the vortex narrowed, Will and Dora were thrown closer together. Will tried to grab hold of Dora. But he was unable to maneuver his arms in the racing swirl of wind.

At first there was nothing but blackness as they fell. Below them, however, was a glimmer of light. Then a strange brightness could be detected as they neared the bottom of the shaft. It was a sterile white light, not like the dim yellow light on the surface.

The wind's vortex began to weaken. Then

suddenly it released them. They fell in a heap to the bottom of the shaft.

It took several minutes for Will to recover. His body ached from the beating it had taken. He sat up and blinked his eyes, trying to accustom them to his new surroundings. He was bathed in light. It stretched from the floor and walls upward some thirty meters before it dissolved in darkness.

He made a rough estimate that they had fallen about a hundred meters. He looked around at the brightly illuminated cave. The space was immense. The floor and walls had a rough texture, like unsmoothed cement. Some strange mineral hung from the walls in stalactites. There were no shadows. Everywhere he looked the white light glimmered. Above them the whirlwind of air continued its motions, gathering in clouds of yellow dust that settled slowly to the bottom of the cave.

He checked the instruments on his space suit. Nothing was damaged. He could breathe easily. But it was much warmer down here.

He reached into a pocket and pulled out his radiometer. The needle was still stretched to the limit, just as it had been when he took a

reading on the surface above. But now he could feel the great strength and intensity of the radio signals. They seemed to be passing through his body. Will looked over at Dora. She lay on the floor without moving.

"Dora!" he called out in alarm. "Are you all right?" He crawled over to her. The aches in his body caused him sharp twinges of pain. There was no response to his calls. Dora's eyelids were closed. He put his head to her chest. The heartbeat was feeble but regular. And she was breathing.

She stirred uneasily and moaned in pain. But she did not regain consciousness. A fine dust continued to fall around them. Will looked around the cave. He could see it more clearly now. It extended about thirty meters from the base of the shaft. The sides sloped down and away. They were clear of the falling dust. He decided to move Dora away from the shaft. If they stayed there any longer the dust might penetrate their oxygenators. They might suffocate.

A strange light glimmers
off the cave walls.

He dragged Dora slowly and carefully away from the shaft to a point where the air was clear. A few moments later, Dora opened her eyes. She struggled to sit up. Will helped her. She blinked her eyes until she became accustomed to the strange light.

"Will," she said. "What happened to us? Where are we? Why is this place so bright?"

Will shook his head. "I don't know. Those surface winds must have formed a whirlpool or funnel system at the opening of the hole. We were sucked down into it. Can you feel how warm it is down here?"

"Yes," she said feebly, still trying to summon up her normal strength. Breathing was difficult. Her ribs and left arm were throbbing with pain.

"The warm air down here must act like a vacuum, drawing in the cooler air above," Will said. "The high winds must have created a reverse tornado effect."

Dora said nothing. She just sat there frowning and cradling her left arm.

"Is your arm broken?" Will asked.

"I don't think so. But it sure hurts like the devil!"

"Try to relax," Will suggested, "at least until we get our bearings. Then we've got to find a way out of here."

"I'm not so sure there is one, Will. It's a long climb to the top. And how could we overcome the force of that wind?" Panic was evident in her eyes. "This is a great way to end the Callisto mission—in our own private prison!" Then suddenly she remembered something. "Will! The communicator! Tell Captain Milo what's happened to us!" She was fully alert now, and so was Will.

Will reached for his communicator. But when he pressed the button, all he could hear was heavy static. Beneath the noise he could detect the pattern of the strange radio signals that had brought them here. The signals were now so powerful that all communication was jammed. There was no way they could get through to Captain Milo.

Back at *Elsa*'s landing point, Captain Milo was becoming impatient. What was the delay in communication? Where had the cadets gone off to? It had been more than an hour since he had heard from Will or Dora.

His thoughts turned to Morrisey's report of a few minutes ago. There had been another message from the Saturn spaceship. The Saturn Patrol was a new venture, a new frontier for the Space Patrol Fleet. It was only a few months ago that the Saturn spaceship had begun orbiting the giant planet. They had reported several blackouts over the last month, before they were told to turn back. Milo made a mental note to check the Saturn report again when they returned to *Alpha*. He wanted to know the orbital position of the spaceship when the last blackout had occurred.

He looked again at his watch, his impatience increasing. What the devil had happened to Will and Dora? He reached for his communicator.

"Captain Milo to Controller Morrisey. Do you read me?"

Morrisey responded almost at once.

"I read you, Captain."

"Morrisey," he said. "Pachek and Johnson have not reported in for more than an hour. Have they tried to make contact with *Alpha*?"

"No, sir. But they would contact you first, no matter what the problem is."

"Yes, of course. Unless for some reason

they couldn't make surface contact. God only knows what kind of electrical disturbances we'll find here. Not to mention the wind, which is fierce. You should be down here, Morrisey. You'd find it exhilarating!"

Morrisey restrained a chuckle.

"What's the plan, Captain? Do you want assistance?"

"Not yet. I'm going to rocket to Point X, where they began their exploration. Stand by for further instructions. That's all!"

"Roger, Captain." All humor was gone from Morrisey's voice. The seriousness of the situation was evident. The space cadets were either lost or dead. He hoped not the latter.

Captain Milo pressed the accelerator on his rocket belt and vaulted into the atmosphere. In less than thirty minutes he located the exact spot where Will had reported landing. As he descended slowly, he circled the area looking for signs of the space cadets. Nothing. But when he landed on the surface, he saw their rocket belts only a few meters away. He also sighted the hole they had reported, some hundred meters beyond.

He walked over to the rocket belts. Why

had they removed them? Then he saw footsteps outlined in the frosty surface. They went off in the direction of the distant hole. He also noticed something else.

The winds were much fiercer here. And above the distant hole was a swirling yellow cloud. He approached cautiously. When he had advanced fifty meters, he stopped. He was bent forward by the wind. It was pulling him in the direction of the hole. He knelt down and took another reading on his radiometer. The needle was straining beyond the absolute limit. The electromagnetic force was unbelievable. They had expected a sharp increase in electromagnetic activity in this section of Callisto and heavy turbulent winds, but nothing of this magnitude.

The turbulence above the hole troubled him. It was like nothing he had ever seen before. He reached down, pried loose a clod of frost-caked soil, and hurled it high into the wind. In seconds it was swallowed up and pulled down into the hole. With a shudder he realized what must have happened to Will and Dora. They had been swallowed up by the wind and forced into the hole. There could be no other explanation of their disappearance. He had surveyed a wide area before he landed at Point X. There was no sign of them other than their rocket belts and the footprints.

Milo watched the swirling winds over the hole. The force could have killed them. He retreated a few steps and thought for a moment. Then he turned back in the direction of *Elsa* and switched on his rocket belt. *Alpha*'s crew had to be alerted.

In the depths of the hole, Will and Dora huddled together. They sat in silence. Their faces betrayed their feeling of doom. Then Dora spoke.

"Will, is there *anything* we can do to let Captain Milo know where we are?"

"Not without the communicator," Will said.

Dora got up slowly and walked over to the wall of the cave. She ran her gloved hand over the surface and pulled loose a chunk of the mineral. As she did so, some granules slid down to the floor.

"If this were gold and we had a way of getting out of here, we'd be rich!" she exclaimed. But her burst of excitement soon faded. Will continued to sit staring into nothingness.

"Isn't there any way we can signal Captain Milo or *Alpha?*"

"How?" Will asked. "The communicator is

jammed with static. It would be like a whisper in a waterfall."

"We've got to think of something!" Dora cried. "We've got to try to find a way out!"

Dora pulls a chunk of mineral loose from one of the cave walls.

7
HOPE IS NOT ENOUGH

Captain Milo spoke sharply into the communicator. "Morrisey! Do you read me?"

"I read you, Captain. Have you found them?"

"No, I haven't. But I've found their rocket belts. Evidently they took them off before they went to look at that hole. And I'm afraid that hole is the answer."

"What do you mean, sir?"

"I mean there's a tornado raising havoc down here. And it's centered above that hole! Every bit of dust and debris that it can gather is being sucked in and shoved down that hole. Has radar-compute picked up the tornado?"

"The entire landing area is full of turbulence, Captain. But we've had no reading for a tornado."

"Maybe because this particular tornado is nqt tunneling *up* into the atmosphere. It's tunneling *down!* Into that hole, like a whirlpool! There must be an electromagnetic attraction inside the hole causing it."

"Do you think Johnson and Pachek are in that hole, Captain?"

"I'm almost sure of it. There's not a sign of them anywhere else. Now listen. Here's what I want you to do. Bring *Elsa* back to the ship. Load it with cable and harness—and some explosives. The N23 bombs should do it. We've got to blast that tornado out of there before we even attempt to look for the cadets. Send Farragut and Orestes down to assist. If we can break up that tornado, I'm going to send Orestes into the hole with the cable. If the cadets are down there, we'll bring them up. That's all!"

Morrisey summoned Farragut and Radames. Soon everything was ready for the rescue attempt. As *Elsa* lay in *Alpha*'s mooring, Morrisey and Kris walked with Farragut and Radames to the docking platform. Morrisey kept his voice calm. But Kris had difficulty concealing her alarm.

"Good luck, Rad," she said. "I hope you find Will and Dora."

"We'll do our best," Radames said. But there was no confidence in his voice. They all knew there was a good chance Will and Dora were buried in that hole. It might not even be possible to find their bodies.

"If we can disrupt that tornado or whatever it is, we have a good chance of finding them," Farragut said.

"I just hope you find them *alive*," Kris said. Then she left to return to the Control Chamber.

Morrisey shook hands with Farragut and Radames. "Tell the captain if need be I'm prepared to land *Alpha* on Callisto. If the N23s don't work, we can blast away with *Alpha*'s attack guns, the laserons."

"Thanks, Morrisey. I'll tell him," Farragut said.

Captain Milo watched *Elsa* approach. It came within fifty meters of the hole, then made a wide sweeping circle around it before landing. *Elsa* braked to a stop only ten meters from

Rad looks out the window of Elsa.

where the captain was standing. Spiderlike legs dug firmly into the hard ground. Farragut was the first to leave *Elsa*. His face was grim as he looked toward the hole and the tornado.

"No change?" he asked Milo.

"No. That tornado or whatever it is seems to have found a permanent home. It's probably been there as long as that hole has. Or as long as these winds have been like they are. I know storms can last for months in this area. That's why we've avoided exploration of it. Other areas of Callisto are more friendly. If it hadn't been for those radio signals, we would never have been sent here." He paused a moment and then said, "At least we're certain of one thing."

"What's that, Captain?"

"No one else would be fool enough to establish a space station here—at least if they're anything at all like us. Whatever's causing those radio signals, it's probably not a piece of equipment that's been brought here by anyone else."

"I think you're right, Captain," Farragut said.

Radames made his way to Farragut's side and greeted the captain. Milo nodded at him but continued speaking to Farragut.

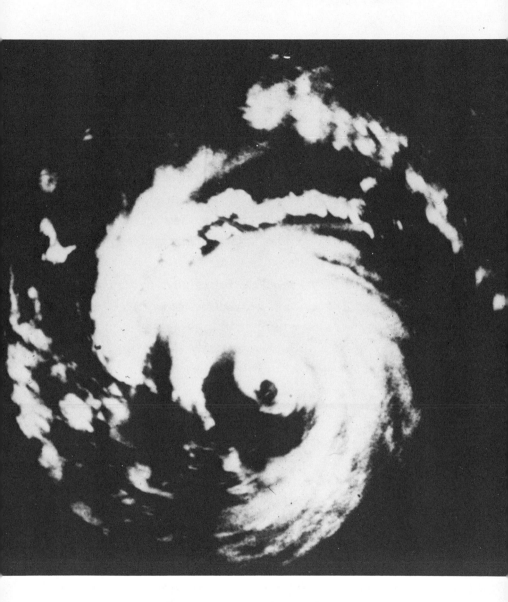

The storm seen from above.

"You have the N23s?"

"Yes, sir. Do you think they're alive, Captain?" asked Farragut.

"I don't know what to think." He turned to Radames. "Get the rocket belts, Orestes. We've got to move and move fast."

"Where will we be placing the bombs, Captain?" Farragut asked.

"I figured a hundred meters north and south of the hole should be just about right. Do you agree?"

"The N23s have a force of twenty tons of nitroglycerine," Farragut stated. "That's enough to clear an area fifty meters wide on the surface. The vertical impact should be at least four times as powerful. It should reach a height of two hundred meters. That should do it."

"We'll find out soon enough," the captain responded. "Let's hope our calculations are correct. Get the bombs."

As Farragut left, Radames approached with the rocket belts. He was straining under the load.

"What should I do with these, Captain?" he asked.

"Put your rocket belt on, Orestes. Put Lieutenant Farragut's belt over there." He pointed to a nearby rise in the ground.

"How many meters of cable did Controller Morrisey put aboard *Elsa?*" the captain asked.

"I think there are two hundred meters," Radames said.

"You *think?*" Captain Milo asked. "Or do you *know?*"

Embarrassed, Radames corrected himself. "There are two hundred meters, sir."

Farragut had returned and was putting on his rocket belt. He came forward and stood at Captain Milo's side.

"Ready, Captain. There are two N23s over there." He indicated the rise where he had found his rocket belt.

"Good!" Captain Milo said. "Does Orestes know how to detonate an N23?"

"I gave him instructions on the flight down, sir."

The captain turned to Radames. "Keep in mind, Orestes, that you'll have only thirty seconds to fly clear of the bomb. You'll set yours off at a point one hundred meters south of the hole. As soon as you press the detonator, take off. Get at least five kilometers south of the point of explosion. Lieutenant Farragut will go to a point one hundred meters north of the hole to set off his N23. Then he'll retreat five kilometers due north. As soon as you two leave, I'll board *Elsa* and take it to a point due east of here, out of range of the blast."

Milo walked over to Farragut and checked his rocket belt and the N23 bomb he had strapped to his chest. It was the size and shape of a large stone. Then he checked Radames.

"All right," he said. "Let's not waste any more time. Remember, wait for my signal before you set the bombs off. They must go off simultaneously. We've got to hit that funnel cloud from both sides at the same time. The impact should break the funnel's tension and send the wind force off in different directions. If we've figured it right, it'll work. If not, these bombs will build a mountain over that hole. Now, off you go!"

Farragut and Radames vaulted into the sky. Captain Milo boarded *Elsa* and briefed Morrisey on their plans. Moments later, *Elsa* touched the surface at a point safely out of range. When Farragut reported that he and Radames were in position at the target sites, Captain Milo's voice came back in hard, clear tones, "At the ready, Lieutenant . . . Orestes. When I count to three, press the detonators and clear out of there!"

Seconds later he gave the signal. Sudden flashes of light leaped into the sky. Then there was the sound of thunder rumbling across a wide area. The vibrations set off by the explosions lasted several minutes.

At the bottom of the shaft, Will and Dora sat in silence. They were weary and frustrated. The heat of the cave was starting to penetrate their space suits. They could feel beads of sweat forming on their foreheads. They stared at the gleaming walls that bathed them in the strange fluorescent light. Every few minutes they checked their radiometers. There was no letup in the electromagnetic force. It continued to exceed the maximum reading. Every few minutes they walked to the opening in the shaft and looked up. The wind remained constant.

Even with no wind to overcome, it looked as if it would be impossible to scale the walls and climb out of the hole. The shaft went straight up to the surface, and the sides were smooth. There would be nothing to hang onto. Mountain climbers' picks were not standard equipment on a mission to one of Jupiter's moons.

Hours had passed since they had been captured by the wind and thrown down into the bright prison below. Still no sign of Captain Milo or the others. Was this to be their grave, buried deep below Callisto's surface in a golden vault, like the ancient pharaohs of Egypt? Exhausted by tension and fear, Will and Dora stretched out on the floor of the cave to wait—and hope.

Suddenly they were startled out of their lethargy by a gigantic blast and rolling thunder. Waves of ground shocks followed. A heavy shower of dust and debris fell to the bottom of the shaft, forming a mound. Then everything was quiet again. Will and Dora looked at each other.

"Will, what do you think that was?" Dora asked. "A volcano erupting?"

"It could have been," Will said. "We did pass some mountains on the way here. We'd better brace ourselves for more shock waves."

They waited in silence for what seemed like an eternity but was only a few seconds. There were no more shock waves. But then they heard rumbling sounds again, this time much closer. A crack suddenly tore through the wall behind them. Several chunks of mineral fell to the floor of the cave. They scrambled to their feet and moved over to the base of the shaft. Something was different. They looked up. The light at the top was dim, but the air was clear and quiet.

"Will!" Dora shouted. "The wind is gone! Maybe we have a chance now!"

But as she turned to look up again, a large chunk of mineral fell from the wall directly above her. It struck her head and back and knocked her to the floor. She immediately lost consciousness.

"Dora!!!" Will shouted as he ran to her side. But as he knelt down to see how badly she was hurt, another chunk of mineral fell, this time behind him. He stopped moving and sat motionless. How long, he wondered, would it be before he became the cave's next victim?

He didn't have long to wonder. Even before he had time to finish his thought, another chunk of mineral fell. It hit Will squarely on the forehead. The young cadet felt a stab of pain. Then everything went black.

As soon as the air had cleared after the explosions, Captain Milo brought *Elsa* back to Point X. The funnel cloud was gone.

He hovered above the hole and looked down into its depths. All he could see was a long, dark shaft, with a faint glimmer of light at the end of it. If Johnson and Pachek had fallen to the bottom of that shaft, he thought, it would be a miracle if they were still alive.

He dropped down for a closer look and made a wide circle of the area. Gradually he drew closer to the hole. What he saw alarmed him. There was a deep depression in the ground just south of the hole. There was also a jagged crack that hadn't been there before. The crack, which widened in a path that led directly to the hole, threatened the stability of the area. The shaft could cave in at any moment.

He made an urgent call to Farragut and Radames. He told them to join him at once. Then he landed *Elsa* as close to the hole as he dared.

Within minutes Farragut and Radames were in sight. As they slowed to a landing, they could see Captain Milo standing by *Elsa.* He had attached the cable line to the lander's body and was holding a rope harness in his hands. His face reflected the urgency of the situation.

He wasted no time on greetings. "Lieutenant, I don't know how much longer that shaft will hold. I'm going to send Orestes down and hope to heaven he can find them and bring them up. But we have very little time." He turned to Radames.

"We're going to lower you into that shaft. When you get to the bottom, if you find them, send them up one at a time in the harness. I'll give you an extra length of cable in case you need it.

"You may not find them. Do your best. But don't stay down there any longer than neces-

Above and over:
Captain Milo and
Farragut look down
into the hole.

sary. We should have time for one good attempt. But that's all."

Radames was alarmed. What if the shaft caved in while he was down there? He'd be buried alive! He was almost ready to ask the captain to send Farragut in his place. But this was the kind of unexpected challenge he'd have to face regularly as a cadet. No, he'd have to go. It was his job. There was no escaping it. Strangely, this knowledge gave him courage.

Moments later Radames was slowly lowered into the shaft. He used his gloved hands to keep clear of the sides. As he neared the bottom, he was amazed to see the cave brighten with a fluorescent light. The cracks in the walls of the shaft showed clearly now. Then he saw Will and Dora sprawled in a heap at the bottom of the shaft. Nearby were several chunks of fallen mineral.

He touched bottom and removed the harness. He went to Dora first. She was unconscious and moaning in pain. Radames carefully placed her in the harness. Then he took the extra length of cable, slipped it under her arms, and tied it to the back of the harness. This would give her more support. He pulled on the cable. Dora was slowly lifted to the ground above.

He turned to Will, calling his name. Will stirred and blinked open his eyes.

"Radames! I've been hit," he cried weakly. Then he slipped back into unconsciousness.

In a few moments the empty harness was again lowered to the bottom of the shaft. Getting Will into it was more difficult. Will was larger and heavier than Dora. But eventually Will too was safely strapped in. Some small chunks of mineral fell from the shaft as the harness was raised to the surface. Radames stepped back to avoid being hit.

As he waited for the harness to return, Radames looked around at the brightly illuminated cave. Every few moments there was a low rumble. Small chunks of mineral continued to fall. Radames looked up into the shaft. There were more cracks in the walls now. His nervousness increased again. Then he saw the harness coming back down. He was soon strapped in and on his way up.

By the time he reached the surface, the rumbling below had become continuous. Farragut quickly pulled him out of the harness. They both hurried to *Elsa.* When they looked back, the hole had disappeared.

8
CAPTAIN MILO'S PRIZE

As soon as they were back aboard *Alpha,* Captain Milo notified Space Command of the incident. Medical instructions were issued immediately.

They were then told to continue their surveillance of Callisto, but only from *Alpha,* not on the surface. Captain Milo was to give them a full report in three days. At that time new orders would be issued.

Will soon regained consciousness, but Dora's injuries were more serious. She had suffered a severe head concussion and a badly bruised back. She was put to bed and heavily sedated. Her recovery was slow, and she had only brief spells of consciousness. Kris attended to her needs and gave her medication as directed by the doctor on Mars. The drugs made Dora groggy, and she slept most of the time.

Will had been luckier. His concussion was a mild one, and it was his only serious injury. The bruises he had suffered healed quickly. In a few days he was fully recovered.

When he reported to Captain Milo for the daily briefing, however, he noted a change in the crew's mood. All except Dora, who remained on the sick list, were present.

"I've just given Space Command a full report on the mission," Milo was saying. "They know that every kilometer of Callisto has been electronically searched. Of course we looked for any sign of an installation that might be causing the radio signals. Nothing was found. We believe the answer is somewhere around Point X. Pachek and Johnson led us to that spot. But that's where the search ends. We think we know *where,* but we don't know why or how." He paused a moment, then continued.

"I think you should know how unimpressed Space Command was with our news. We've been ordered to return to Mars, mission unaccomplished." The captain's harsh tone made Will flinch.

"With the collapse of the shaft, we lost our chance to explore that cave again. We don't have the equipment or the crew for a major excavation.

"We did prove one thing, however. Manned landings can be made on Callisto in spite of the wind turbulence. But as to the radio signals, another mission will have to solve that mystery. That is, if Space Command thinks it's worth the trouble or expense."

They were dismissed, feeling for the first time the full impact of the mission's failure. Will, Radames, and Farragut left the Control Chamber. The captain had assigned Will and Radames to work in the Exobiology Lab.

Kris and Morrisey remained behind on Captain Milo's orders. Kris began monitoring radar-compute. Morrisey sat down at a desk to complete the day's flight report. They worked in silence. Captain Milo's mood did not encourage conversation.

After a long interval, the captain himself broke the quiet. "Take over, Morrisey. I'm going to look in on Johnson." The sliding plastiglass door opened, and he walked through to the elevator. Within seconds he had arrived at Dora's room.

As he greeted her, the captain was pleased

to note that the color had returned to Dora's face. Her eyes looked alert.

"Good to see you awake, Johnson," he said. "The last time I looked in you were in slumberland."

He sat down beside her bed. "Winter showed me your medical report this morning. For the first time since we brought you up from the cave, your blood pressure is normal. So is your pulse. And from the look of your breakfast request, I'd say your appetite is fine too. Ready to go back to work?"

Dora smiled. "I'm ready, Captain. Just don't give me anything heavy to lift—for a while anyway. But I can use the gray matter!"

Then she pointed to her space suit that had been folded and left on a chair. "Captain, reach into the left pocket of my suit," she said. "There's something I've been wanting to give you."

The captain walked over to the chair. As he reached into the suit pocket, he pulled out a small clump of mineral. He marveled to see its fluorescent glow. Even in full light, it glimmered.

"Is this from the cave?" he asked, still studying the clump. "When I relayed Pachek's description of the cave to Space Command, they thought the rock might be a phosphorescent

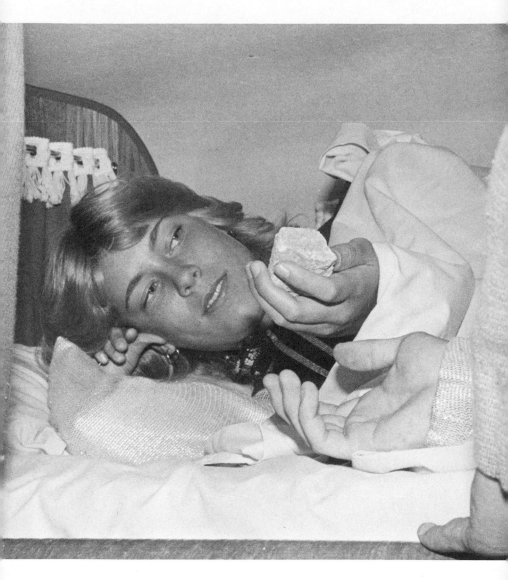

*Dora and Captain Milo discuss
the strange mineral.*

type. Or maybe some mineral with a high sulphur content. But this wouldn't fit that description at all." He weighed the rock in his hands. "It's quite heavy," he said.

Suddenly he reached for his communicator. "Farragut! Morrisey! Report to Johnson's room at once! Repeat. Report to Johnson's room at once!"

He was still holding the mineral in his hands when Farragut and Morrisey arrived. "What's up, Captain?" Morrisey asked.

"This is up," he said, holding out the mineral so they could take a closer look. "It's a little souvenir that Johnson was clever enough to pocket before that shaft caved in.

"From what Pachek has told us so far, this may be quite a prize." He turned to Dora.

"Johnson, I commend you. You've given us something, at least, to show for this mission." Then he turned to Farragut. "Lieutenant, I want you to analyze the mineral." He looked at Dora. "Would you like to assist? Do you feel up to it, Johnson?"

"You won't have to ask me twice, Captain." As she spoke, she started to lift herself from the bed. "If you men will leave for a minute, I'll get into my lab clothes."

Captain Milo gently pushed her back down.

"Hold on, Johnson. You're not as strong as you think. We don't want a relapse. Winter will help you get used to walking again. A day or two of light exercise should do the trick. Then, if you feel strong enough, you can join Lieutenant Farragut."

Dora's desire to work on the project helped speed her recovery. She teetered a bit during her walks with Kris the first day and had a few dizzy spells. But by the end of the second day she was much steadier. Captain Milo gave her permission to go to work.

She started working half-days, but soon was at Farragut's side all day long and sometimes into the evening. Although there was excitement over the project, their early experiments revealed little. Then they discovered something that made their eyes pop.

They tried to reach Captain Milo at once. He was on his way to the Exobiology Lab to observe Will and Radames, they were told. Captain Milo was just opening the door to the lab when he saw Farragut running toward him, followed closely by Dora.

"Captain!" Farragut shouted excitedly. "We just tried to reach you in the Control Chamber. Can you come with us a moment? We have some data that may surprise you."

"What kind of surprise, Lieutenant?"

"We'll let you be the judge."

They entered the lab where Farragut and Dora had been working. The Lieutenant led the way to a clear plastiglass chamber sitting on top of the lab's only table. On the front of the chamber were a series of dials. Inside, resting on a tray, was the mineral from the cave.

"We've put this sample through exhaustive tests, Captain," Farragut began. "We've broken down the elements and tested it for radioactivity. But it wasn't until today that we made an important discovery. This mineral, Captain, *is* the source of those radio signals!"

"What? Are you sure, Farragut?"

"Well, we need to make more tests, Captain. Those can be done when we get back to Space Station Mars. They have the equipment there we need to be certain. But we have a pretty good idea how the elements break down. This sample contains iron, silicon, hydrogen, and helium. That's not surprising in itself. Not at that depth below Callisto's surface. What is surprising is the electromagnetic force of this mineral. It's stronger than anything known.

"I've made some preliminary tests, Captain. I'd say it's strong enough to send radio signals even to the outermost planets, including Pluto." Farragut motioned to Dora. "Johnson has been studying the mineral's radioactivity. Tell Captain Milo what you've found."

Dora began. "Well, Captain, the mineral's strength is not in its radioactivity. If it were, Will and I would have been dead by the time you found us. We were surrounded by that mineral. We could feel its power. And it was strong enough to jam the communicators.

"It seems to be powered by some form of cosmic ray. We know cosmic rays travel at the speed of light. They can travel in a straight line millions of kilometers into space—"

Captain Milo interrupted her. "What direction did those signals show on your radiometers when you and Pachek were in the cave?"

"The reading was 15 degrees northeast, sir."

"That explains it," Milo said.

"Explains what, Captain?" Farragut asked.

"It explains why radar-compute blacked out on the Saturn spaceship, Lieutenant. I made a note of its position when it reported the blackout. At that position in Saturn's orbit, the spaceship would be in a direct line 15 degrees northeast of Point X on Callisto."

9
HOMECOMING

In the distance the friendly red planet brightened in the solar sun. Just a few more days and *Alpha* would be in its home mooring, in the docking platform above Space Station Mars.

For the first time in all the months of the Callisto mission, Captain Milo was relaxed. He was smiling broadly and happily. Space Command had just sent him the preliminary findings on the strange mineral.

There was a chance, he told them, that the mineral would revolutionize space communications. It might even provide a new source of energy. Space Command would be ordering complete tests on the sample rock as soon as they landed on Mars.

"Callisto may be one more member of our solar system that will prove useful to humanity," the captain told them. "True, it's cold and stormy. It won't be easy to excavate there or do full-scale mining operations. Not with those turbulent winds. But that's what Space Command intends to do, if that mineral proves as valuable as they think it is."

That small chunk of rock had made all the difference. Their mission had been a huge success.

This time the captain didn't end the briefing with a curt dismissal. Instead he said, "This calls for a celebration." He went over to the meal control dial. "How do you like your steaks?" he asked.

"Rare for me," said Dora. "Like that Callistan mineral!"

Laughing, they all left the Control Chamber for the dining area.

Relaxing in the cadet lounge after dinner, Will chose a seat next to Kris.

"Where do you think we'll go next?" Kris asked.

"Probably to get some good old R and R— Rest and Relaxation!" he leaned back in his

chair. "And then another mission, maybe to Saturn."

"I wonder if we'll be together again," Kris thought out loud.

"I hope so," Will said. "I think we make a good team. *All* of us." He looked across the room to where Farragut, Dora, and Radames were sitting. Radames looked older, more confident. He was a rookie no longer.

Dora and Farragut were talking. Their minds were filled with thoughts of the mineral. Radames suddenly cut in.

"I can't get those radio signals out of my head," he said to Farragut. "It was almost as if they were in code."

"I know," Farragut answered. "But it wasn't a code. Just power. Power that we may be able to use to stretch the frontiers of outer space. And that's a lot more exciting, somehow, than a secret code."

"Lieutenant," Dora said, "Captain Milo said you'd been assigned to Project Radiant." That

Dora and Farragut discuss the mineral, while Rad puzzles over the "signals" it sends out.

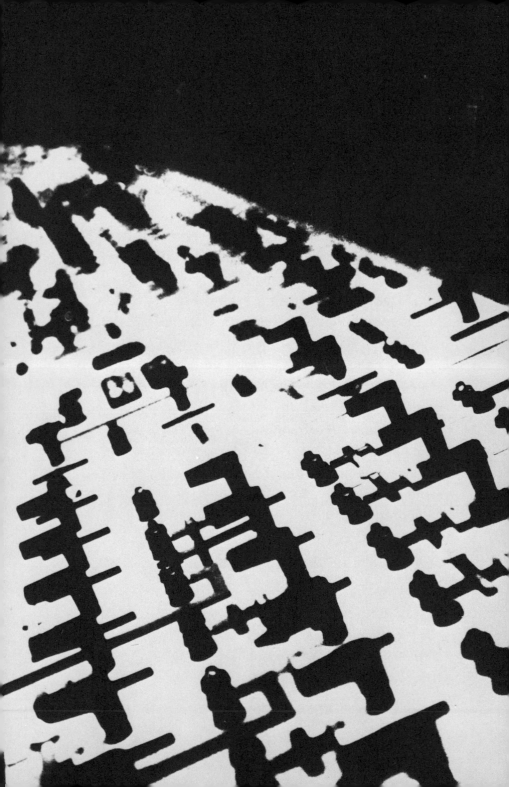

was the name given to the research project that would study the new mineral.

"That's right. Like to join us, Dora? I might be able to get you assigned to the project."

"Well," she said thoughtfully, "up to now my specialty has been exobiology." Then she grinned. "But yes. I'd jump at the chance!"

Farragut smiled. Just then a voice blared over the intercom. It was Morrisey.

"Captain Milo wants you to know that we've just passed through the Asteroid Belt. This time, no bumps. Next stop, Mars! Prepare for homecoming, cadets!"

Alpha *heads for home—*
mission accomplished.

ABOUT
THE AUTHOR

Robert E. Dunbar is a former assistant professor of scientific communications at the University of Health Sciences/the Chicago Medical School and is now a free-lance writer. Though he has done several books in the science field for Franklin Watts, this is his first work of fiction.

Mr. Dunbar is married to a teacher and artist. They live with their two children in Nobleboro, Maine.